Schools
A Niche Market for Authors

Jane R. Wood

Jacksonville, Florida

Publisher's Cataloging-In-Publication

Wood, Jane R., 1947–
Schools: a niche market for authors / Jane R. Wood.

p. : ill. ; cm.

Issued also as an ebook.
Includes bibliographical references.

ISBN: 978-0-9863325-4-8
Library of Congress Number: 2013951416

1. Authorship-Marketing. 2. Teaching—Aids and devices—Marketing.
I. Title.

Z285.6.W66 2014
070.50688

Cover image: Thinkstockphotos.com/frimage

Florida Kids Press
11802 Magnolia Falls Drive
Jacksonville, FL 32258
904-268-9572

www.janewoodbooks.com

Printed in USA

Dedication

To all the educators who have invited authors into their schools to connect with and inspire their students.

Contents

Acknowledgments

I am deeply indebted to the hundreds of educators who have welcomed me into their schools and shared my books with their students. A few have been quoted or photographed in this book, including Linda Smigaj, Malisa Pellicer, Clare Dubase, Brett Ovcen, Michelle Cates, and Donna Ayers, and my thanks extend to all the teachers I've worked with over the past seventeen years.

I also wish to recognize other authors who have shared some of their techniques with me regarding their school presentations, the additional resources they've developed for their books, and the names of schools that are interested in connecting with authors. Several who have been especially helpful are Frances Keiser, Marianne Berkes, Darrell House, and Mark Wayne Adams.

My sincere appreciation also goes to my team of colleagues at Get Book Savvy, a company that helped authors simplify the process of publishing and marketing their books. Thanks and kudos to Frances Keiser, Kathy Shea, and Beth Mansbridge. Their guidance, expertise, and friendship continue to be invaluable to me.

Special thanks to graphic designer Elizabeth Blacker, who has formatted all of my juvenile fiction books, designed all the book covers, and updated the content of this book in 2017 and in 2021.

I especially want to acknowledge all the young readers who have read my books. They are the reason I write them; why I visit schools; and why I want to see other authors connecting with them. As Dr. Seuss put it:

"The more that you read, the more things you will know. The more that you learn, the more places you'll go."

This book is to encourage all authors to take young readers to new places.

Introduction

Schools are a unique market for authors. Whether it's a children's picture book, a chapter book, a young adult book, or even an adult fiction or nonfiction book, the goal for most authors is the same—to sell books.

As the author of five juvenile fiction books, I've been selling my books to schools since 2004. More than 50 percent of my annual revenue comes from book sales to schools, fees from speaking at schools, and book sales to students at those schools. It's a win-win-win.

However, there is also a valuable benefit to the schools. As a former teacher, I want to get kids reading. By creating characters that kids can relate to and scenes that engage their interest and imagination, I am also promoting literacy. When I participate in an author visit to a school, I'm making a connection with my readers—something beneficial to both of us. And when I talk about the writing process to students, I am reinforcing what their teachers are telling them in their language arts classes.

When targeting schools as a market for your books, there are numerous things to consider. In this book I will share many of the strategies I have used successfully in making my books attractive to educators:

- How I promote my books to schools;
- How I develop my presentations; and
- How I am able to generate revenue from this niche market.

Chapter 1

Preparing a Book
for the School Market

DEVELOPING BOOKS WITH EDUCATIONAL VALUE

The most critical criteria to consider when marketing your books to schools is that the books must have educational value.

There are thousands of cute children's books written each year, especially now, with the popularity of self-publishing. However, authors need to realize that class time is a valuable commodity to teachers. With stress being put on standardized tests, emphasis on state standards, and add to that district-level expectations, teachers must focus on resources that are compatible with the curriculum they are expected to teach.

The solution is simple. A book that will be popular for classroom use with teachers and media specialists must reinforce what is being taught. School budgets are tight, as are their daily schedules. Educators must justify where they spend the school's money and their classroom time.

I've written five juvenile fiction books, aimed at young readers ages 8-14. As a former teacher, I weave history, information about the environment, and some interesting facts into stories filled with mystery, adventure, and humor. Kids like my books because they're fun. Teachers like them because they have many "teachable moments," as one teacher put it.

Books that are cross-curricular, meaning they reinforce more than one subject area such as history, geography, math, or science, make them even more valuable for classroom use. Nonfiction books have become increasingly more desirable for schools because of the emphasis that state standards places on students' understanding of informational texts.

However, authors do not need to be former teachers to have their books considered for classroom use—but their books do need to have educational value. In this book I will discuss several ways an author can do that. If a story or book does not reinforce some of the core curricula, then it's going to be a hard sell to schools.

"My students love Jane Wood's books. They're full of adventure and fun, but they also teach the children many things about our history and the environment. It's a great way for me to make connections to the other things we're studying."

—Linda Smigaj, National Board Certified Teacher in Literacy

Books That Are Appropriate

Another factor for school consideration is the appropriateness of the content. Language, situations, or themes that are questionable are cause for rejection. Even though many kids today use colorful language and purchase books that reflect their standards, it's the teachers, administrators, literacy coaches, and media specialists who will be making the purchasing decisions for schools.

When I wrote the manuscript for my first book, *Voices in St. Augustine*, I ended chapter one with the phrase "history sucks," as that aptly described the thoughts of the 13-year-old boy who was just assigned a history project. Before I went to print with the book, I had several elementary school teachers review the manuscript.

A large part of my target audience is third, fourth, and fifth graders, so getting teacher input was an important step. (I suggest all authors who intend to market their books to schools have their manuscripts reviewed by teachers.)

All of the teachers told me their district would not allow my book in their schools if I used the word "sucks," even though that was the exact word kids would use in that situation. I changed the phrase to "history stinks" and have sold thousands of copies of that book to schools.

Developing Educational Resources

It is not difficult for me, as a former teacher, to develop educational resources to accompany my books. When I was teaching I found it was much easier to motivate students in a learning activity if it was fun. I'd create games and word puzzles that reinforced what we were studying.

On my author website I include resources for teachers and activities for students for each of my books. By listing vocabulary words and discussion questions by chapter, I make it attractive for teachers to use my books so they won't have to spend a lot of their own time in preparation.

Common Core State Standards were national standards designed to help provide a defined understanding of what students are expected to learn at each grade level. However, many states and districts have developed their own set of standards. Be cognizant of what is being used when developing resources for your book.

However, should you decide to include correlations to state standards as part of your educational resources, you should match the specific standard to the grade levels and subject areas you are targeting.

"Using fiction books is a good way to teach students about descriptive details, context clues, dialogue, and organized structure—all aspects of state standards. When authors provide additional resources that focus on many of those skills, it makes it easier for teachers to incorporate those books into their lesson plans."

—Linda Smigaj, National Board Certified Teacher in Literacy

Authors of nonfiction books should also be aware of the skills identified in the state standards, as there is an increased emphasis on informational texts, including biographies, literary nonfiction, journals, essays, technical manuals, and books with maps, charts, and graphs.

Since most authors are not familiar with the expectations of state standards or district-level standards, I suggest you pay a teacher to develop them for you if you want to offer them as a resource. Many teachers would welcome the extra money, and they would be an ideal person to consult for this. Teachers can be a valuable resource for you in many ways.

Authors of children's books should examine their books as an educator would. What would be suitable for classroom use based on the curricula? Talk to some classroom teachers to determine what subjects the students are studying and what skills are being reinforced.

Many authors envision their books as part of the character education curricula because their story has a moral or a lesson. While that may be true, the reality is that most school districts have little or no funding for character education materials. Although character education may be mandated by the state or district, teachers have told me they are expected to use existing materials that are already available to them.

Also, there are many free resources on character education on the Internet. Some teachers have created their own stories to exemplify the six pillars of character education. For more information on the six pillars, refer to https://charactercounts.org/.

So, having a cute story or a story with a moral is not enough. Content related to science, history, geography, mathematics, or any of the subject areas taught in schools will help position your books for school sales. You might have to do some research to determine what is being taught in any given state or school district. To do that, check out the district or state website and search for pages related to academic programs, curriculum, instruction, assessment, or standards. This can be time well invested when it comes to marketing your books to those schools.

Creating Student Activities

In creating student activities to accompany my books, I try to make it fun, yet challenging and educational. My favorite student activity is the electronic scavenger hunt. I develop a list of ten questions that can be answered by visiting a designated website. The questions and the websites all relate back to the content of the book. Not only do the students learn about the history or ecosystem of the setting of my book, they're also learning how to navigate websites to find specific information.

For younger students there are coloring sheets, mazes, and exercises involving counting, shapes, sizes, colors, and letters. Ideally these worksheets should be embellished with images or characters from the book. Work with your illustrator or graphic designer to develop these. Again, if you're not good at creating these kinds of resources, pay a teacher to help you design them. They would know the kinds of skills that need to be reinforced.

You can also peruse a school supply store or check out some websites that provide these kinds of resources for teachers and parents. However, beware of copyright restrictions. Do not copy something directly from someone else's materials. Use their ideas as a model to help develop your own.

Some authors, especially those of children's picture books, will include resources at the back of their book, like a glossary, photographs, illustrations, a brief history, even discussion questions. When these resources are included as part of the book, it also helps parents and grandparents turn the time spent reading to a child into a learning experience.

Having additional educational resources accompany your books can greatly enhance the chances of schools buying them. It creates credibility for you and your books when you're marketing to schools. If you'd like to see the kinds of resources I offer, go to the Books page on my website, at www.janewoodbooks.com.

Some Personal Experiences

Because my first book, *Voices in St. Augustine,* takes place in St. Augustine, Florida (and Florida history is taught in the fourth grade throughout the state of Florida), I have a built-in market. That was intentional. It has helped me sell many books to schools. And it has helped many teachers make their history lessons more relevant to some fourth graders, especially those like Joey, who think "history stinks." One teacher, Malisa Pellicer, sent me this comment:

> *I am a 4th-grade teacher and I just wanted to tell you how much my students loved* Voices in St. Augustine. *They laughed, predicted, and groaned each afternoon when I said it was time to put the book away. We went to St. Augustine for a field trip and I brought along my copy of* Voices. *When we were on the gun deck of the fort, I grabbed a few kids and pointed north*

to the narrow walkway where Joey takes a walk. They were so excited. Students also had the book open on the trolley, pointing to things they saw that were pictured in the book. Thank you for helping make history come alive for these impressionable 10-year-olds. They will never forget it.

When I wrote my fourth book, *Ghosts on the Coast: A Visit to Savannah and the Low Country,* I chose Savannah and Charleston as the settings. There's some notable history in both of those southern cities—the challenges the early settlers faced, the American Revolution, and the Civil War, to name a few. Because American history is taught in the fifth grade in Florida, many schools buy both of my books to continue using fiction and characters the students are familiar with to teach history at both the fourth and fifth grades. For me, it's a win-win. And this former teacher finds it extremely rewarding to know that I am still having an impact in the classroom.

Chapter 2

Promoting Your Books
to Schools

Developing Print Marketing Materials

One of the first things to do in promoting your books to schools is to develop a flier or brochure about your books. A second flier can be created specifically for school visits. It's smart to have print copies of these so you can hand them to people when making appearances, doing book signings, or at any vendor tables you purchase for selling your books.

One of the most effective marketing strategies is to have those same print materials available as PDF files so they can be attached to an email or included as a link on your website or on social media sites. If you want people to know about your book, having print materials readily available is a good selling strategy. They can learn about you and your book, and even though they may not buy immediately, many of them will keep it for future reference. Sometimes I've had schools place an order for books many months after they received one of my fliers. Often it's a budgeting issue; but because they had my flier, it kept my books on their radar screen.

When creating a flier, I suggest you have it done professionally by a graphic designer and include:

- a short description of the book;
- a cover image;
- the ISBN number;
- the retail price;
- your website and contact information;
- information about ordering;
- information about a distributor or wholesaler, if you have one;
- a short biography, "About the Author"; a photo is optional; and
- any endorsements, excerpts from reviews, or awards the book has received.

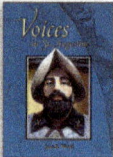

As with all documents you produce for your book, have it edited by a professional copy editor. Using a professional editor is critical. Many authors who are self-publishing today don't use professionals such as editors and graphic designers, and their materials look amateurish. You don't want to be put in that category. Invest the money and do it right for your own benefit.

You might want to consider other promotional items, like bookmarks, postcards, and posters. Don't forget to have some business cards produced as well.

Developing Online Outreach

Another key way to promote your book is through a website. Every author needs a website. Let the website reflect the tone of your book. If it's a children's book, make it colorful. If it's a chapter book, use images that will engage 10-year-olds. And if it's a young adult book, write a description that will stimulate the interest of teenagers. Check out other author websites for ideas.

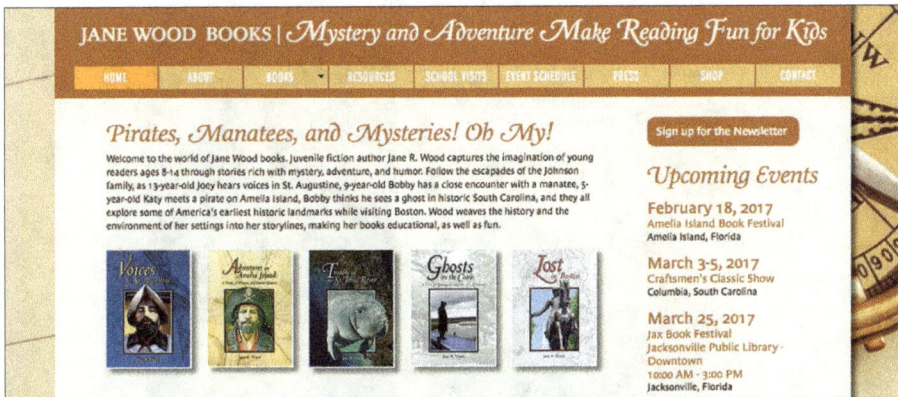

The content for author websites is pretty standard:

- home page;
- author bio with photo;
- a shop or store page where people can order your book;
- a calendar or list of upcoming events in which you'll be participating;
- a photo gallery, optional;
- any educational resources you've developed; and
- information about school visits.

View in your browser

JANE WOOD BOOKS
Mystery and Adventure Make Reading Fun for Kids

August Newsletter

Accelerated Reader® Program

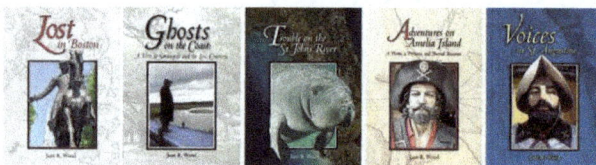

All five of my chapter books are now a part of the **Accelerated Reader®** program. Many schools use this program to encourage students to read. The point value, interest level, and book reading level for each of my books are listed on my website at janewoodbooks.com and on the AR BookFinder™ website.

A+ Book List

My books are also a part of the A+ Book List
reviewed by publishing profes... ...rica,
educators, students... ...A+ Book List
classroom... ...rican Library Association
... ...e in Orlando.

BookExpo America in Chicago

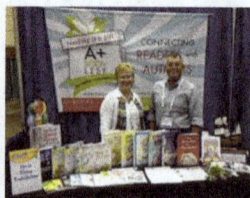

American Library Association in Orlando

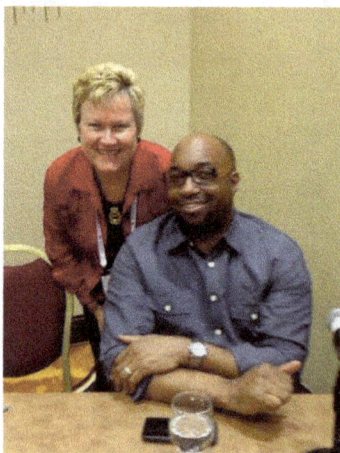

Publishing University in Salt Lake City

Jane R. Wood can be contacted at
jane@janewoodbooks.com **or 904-268-9572**

It's fairly easy today to develop your own website. You need at least a basic presence on the Internet. However, if designing a website is not your area of competency, I suggest you pay someone to develop a professional-looking one for you. Having a website is critical. It will expand your exposure far beyond your local marketing efforts, and provide a way for people to learn about your book, contact you, and order your book. I can't say this enough—having a website is a must.

Another way to stimulate good exposure for your book is to write a periodic e-newsletter or blog. For that, you need a good distribution list. At all my school visits, book signings, or appearances, I provide a sign-up sheet for my e-newsletter. Whenever I meet someone who expresses an interest in my books, I ask if they'd like to be added to my distribution list. (It's not good protocol to add someone to a distribution list unless they request it.)

With many e-newsletter programs, you can separate your contacts into categories. Creating a category for educators means you can customize messages that you might want to send to them periodically, like announcing the launch of a new book, the addition of a new resource on your website, or a special date that relates to your book.

For example, I like to remind teachers about *Talk Like a Pirate Day* each September 19, as it gives me an opportunity to tie it back to my book, *Adventures on Amelia Island: A Pirate, a Princess, and Buried Treasure*. Each spring I promote Earth Day events and activities and suggest teachers have their students read *Trouble on the St. Johns River*, which has an environmental theme.

I don't overwhelm my contacts with multiple communications, but reserve the privilege for times when I have something to say. Many times I will receive book orders or requests to schedule a school visit after one of my e-newsletters has been sent. It's a way of reminding my contacts about me and my books.

Networking

Networking in person is another positive way to gain entree to schools. If you've identified some schools where you'd like to sell your books, then check out their calendar of events. If there's a literacy night or reading festival, volunteer to participate by promoting reading. They may ask you to speak and often will allow you to sell your books.

If a school has a fall carnival or holiday arts and crafts show, apply to be a vendor. Often, schools or parent groups will sponsor such events as fund-raisers. These are ideal places to sell your books, as the parents will be attending with their kids.

Whenever you are exhibiting your books, create an enticing display as a vendor. I have small items related to pirates, manatees, sea turtles, and ghosts—all content related to my books—that are like magnets to kids. Think how retail stores promote their wares.

I also like to attend education conferences so I can meet educators and tell them about my books. Most states have conferences for media specialists, reading associations, teacher groups related to grade levels or subject areas, and administrators. Parent organizations have state meetings as well. Ideally, I like to be a presenter at one of these events. The deadline for submissions to present is usually many months before the event, so you must do some online research and plan ahead. Check out national events, as well.

Of course, you must have an appropriate presentation, and are often required to pay for your own expenses. If you're lucky, they will cover your registration, lodging, and sometimes, travel. It will depend on the value of what you have to offer.

Certainly if there is a conference in your area, you should take advantage of the opportunity to attend. Or you can purchase a vendor space in their exhibit area. Vendor fees will vary depending on the size of the conference. Ask other authors if they've participated in the past to determine if the expense is worth it for you.

With any of these events or opportunities, you should be prepared to promote and discuss your book succinctly. Practice your elevator speech, a well-rehearsed statement that tells people about your book in a short amount of time. Making it clever will help them remember you.

When people ask me what I do, I tell them I make history come alive for kids. Almost always they will ask how I do that. I've piqued their interest enough for them to want to learn more about me. That's when I can tell them about my books and how I weave history into stories filled with adventure, mystery, and humor. My response to them is much more interesting than simply saying I write kids' books. When you're trying to make connections for your books, you want people to remember you. It's just good marketing.

Chapter 3

Contacting Schools

One School at a Time

Authors often ask me how I get my books in schools. The answer is simple—one school at a time. However, the process to do that is not so simple.

Many people assume that they simply need to find someone at the administrative level of a school district who deals with their subject matter or targeted grade levels, but that's not the way it works. It's a good idea to introduce yourself, either in person or electronically, to those persons so they are familiar with you and your book—but don't expect them to promote your book throughout their network.

Offer to send them a free copy of your book and ask if they would like to be included on any email or newsletter distribution lists you have. Try to nurture a positive relationship with them, as they can be a good source of information for you by informing you about trends in their district, upcoming events, and new programs being implemented in their district or state.

For me, the first step in selling books to a school is to schedule an author visit. (I will discuss how to prepare for an author visit in Chapter 4.) The best way to connect with individual schools is to find someone at that school who likes your book. You should ask them to help you schedule an author visit. It might be a teacher, a media specialist, a literacy coach, an administrator, or even a parent. Maybe it's someone you know, or a friend of someone you know, or someone you met at a book signing.

Another way to connect with new schools is to utilize your connections at existing schools. Media specialists and teachers have colleagues at other schools. Ask them to recommend you to their friends. Word of mouth is one of the best marketing strategies when trying to expand into any market.

When I want to make a connection for an author visit in a district where I have no contacts, I go to the school district website. I first identify schools within a certain geographic area, making it convenient for me to visit several schools easily during my time there. By going to individual school websites, I also identify schools with larger enrollments. I'll sell more books at a school that has six fourth-grade classes than at a school that has only two.

Next, I try to identify which schools are "A" schools or the equivalent of that. Those are schools where you usually have more parent involvement and more students are likely to purchase copies of your books. Most state department of education websites will list grades or rankings of the schools in their state. Many schools will proudly proclaim that they are an "A" school on their website. It takes some time to do this research, but it can be valuable information when you're targeting schools to contact.

However, don't ignore Title 1 schools. Title 1 schools receive government funding because they have a high percentage of students from low-income families. I have had some of my most meaningful author visits in schools where the students are economically challenged. You will find some of the most creative, dedicated teachers and administrators in those schools. As a former teacher, I welcome the opportunity to visit them. And often, Title 1 schools have budgets to purchase classroom sets of your book.

I also check out a school's mascot. My second book, *Adventures on Amelia Island: A Pirate, a Princess, and Buried Treasure,* has a pirate on the cover and talks about the pirate history of Amelia Island. Whenever I find a school that has a pirate as their mascot, I contact them.

Once I've identified a school via their website, the first person I try to contact is the media specialist. They are usually the ones who will schedule an author visit. Frequently, their email address is listed on the website. If not, call the school and ask to speak to the media specialist.

If you can't identify the media specialist, look for a reading specialist or administrator or a specific classroom teacher. Often, school websites will include individual teacher or class websites. Peruse some of them and you might find a teacher or class that demonstrates an interest in your content area. If they're studying the environment and your book is nature-related, that could be a good connection for you.

After You Establish a School Contact

Once you've made a contact at a school and they express interest in your book, offer to send them a free copy if they're not familiar with it. I realize this will cost you, both the value of the book and postage, but you must think of it as part of your marketing budget. I have found I usually get a good return on that initial investment.

Author Visits to Schools
by Author Jane R. Wood

Do some of your students find history boring? Do you have trouble getting boys to read? Would you like your students to become more aware of the environment? Then I can help.

In my hour-long Author Visit, I spend the first 30 minutes talking about how and why I write my books and how I do the research. I then focus on the writing process, with special emphasis on editing and re-writing. As a published author, I give them a unique perspective on how the writing skills they're learning in school apply to the real world.

I also share photographs and anecdotes about the people, places and animals featured in my books. I then devote 15 minutes to answer their questions, and leave 15 minutes at the end to sign and personalize books for students who want to purchase their own copies.

Your students will discover how history can be part of an adventure, and why concern for endangered animals inspires young people to want to "do something" to make a difference.

My visit is much more meaningful for the students if they have read one of my books before I present. Schools may purchase my books at a discount when ordered directly from me at www.janewoodbooks.com. For students who want to purchase their own copies, I can e-mail you a form that you can send home to parents in advance of my visit.

Teacher Resources
My website contains numerous teacher resources, including Vocabulary Words, Discussion Questions, Correlations to Standards, Links to websites relevant to each book, as well as some student activities like Word Scrambles and Electronic Scavenger Hunts. You can find these resources at www.janewoodbooks.com.

Please contact me directly at 904-268-9572 or jane@janewoodbooks.com, if you are interested in scheduling an Author Visit to your school. Feel free to coordinate with other schools in your area, as I will be glad to pro-rate travel expenses if an Author Visit is scheduled in the same area within the same week.

Fill out this form using your computer, then use the submit button below to email it to jane@janewoodbooks.com or print the form and fax it to 904-268-8165, if you are interested in scheduling an Author Visit:

School Name: _____ City: _____ State: _____

Contact Person: _____ Phone: _____

E-mail address: _____

Fees
(For schools outside the Jacksonville, Florida area.)

❑ **Half-day:**
Two one-hour sessions
$350
plus travel expenses.

❑ **All day:**
Four one-hour sessions
$600
plus travel expenses.

In addition to having a marketing flier about your book, you should also consider creating a flier about your author visits. It should include:

- a description of your book, focusing on its educational value;
- a description of what you do during your presentation;
- your speaking fees;
- any discounts you offer on your books to schools;
- any educational resources you've developed;
- your website;
- your contact information, including both email address and phone number;
- endorsements from educators; and
- any awards the book has received.

This is probably a good place to talk about speaking fees. Many authors who are just starting out will do school visits for free, and that's not a bad idea. That's how I got started, and it's a good way to get your foot in the door.

Today I charge $350 for a half-day visit (two sessions) and $600 for a full day (four sessions). Most authors base their fees or honorariums on their years of experience and the number of books they've published. Check out other authors' websites to see the range of fees being charged.

You can also create a packet of information similar to a press kit, but specifically designed for educators. You need to have these resources readily available should a school ask for them. It could include:

- a flier or brochure about your book;
- a flier about your author visit;
- your author bio, with a photo of you;
- any educational resources you've developed;

- copies of book reviews that would be of interest to educators;
- copies of any news articles that mention your book's educational value; and
- copies of any news articles that might show you interacting with students.

Ask teachers who have read your book or, better yet, those who have used it in their classrooms, to write you an endorsement. These are the types of items that will encourage other educators to want to schedule an author visit with you.

Also, you might want to have the Lexile measures done on your books. Lexiles measure the difficulty of the text, and many schools use them to determine at what grade level or to which students a book is most appropriate. I've had some schools ask me for the Lexile measures on my books before they would consider them. For information on having your text measured, go to: http://www.lexile.com/analyzer/.

Another positive selling point with many schools is if a book is included on reader programs like *Accelerated Reader* (AR). One way that books are added to the AR program is when a school suggests it. If you're working with a school that likes your book, ask them to suggest that your title be added to the AR program. Refer to the Accelerated Reader website at https://www.renaissance.com/ and go to *Suggest a Quiz* under the *Resources* section.

Once a school expresses interest in your book, ask for an opportunity to do an author visit to their school. You can send them a copy of your author visit flier, if you have one. If you don't have one, you'll need to specify what you do during your presentation, how long your presentation lasts, and your fees.

The flier I've created about my author visits can be emailed or mailed to them. Email is a good way to send it because then they can forward it to any other persons who may be decision makers regarding your visit. Remember, your audience is students. Design any description of your presentation to include the things that students will learn from you. It's got to offer more than just the opportunity to meet a "real" author.

- Will you talk about how you get your ideas for the book, hopefully stimulating students with their writing?
- Will you discuss the writing process, or how you do research, or how the illustrations are created?
- Will you elaborate on content from the book that reinforces what they are studying?
- Do you have some special expertise or experience that makes you an intriguing guest speaker for the students?

In addition to endorsements from other educators, photographs of you presenting at other schools and interacting with students are good selling points. Always take a camera with you when you're visiting a school and ask someone to take photos of you during your presentation. It's a good

idea to avoid capturing any students' faces unless the school has a blanket release that their students can be photographed. Taking a picture from the back of the room usually works. Share these photos on your book website, on any social media that you frequent, and include some in your educator packet.

Often, schools will include a photo or article about your visit in their next school newsletter. It's a good idea to email them a photo of you and the cover image of your book prior to your visit. Sometimes they'll create a poster promoting your upcoming author visit. Ask for a copy of any newsletters in which you appear so you can share that with other schools in your educator packet.

If it is appropriate, contact the local media about your visit. When I launched my fourth book, *Ghosts on the Coast: A Visit to Savannah and the Low Country,* I visited several schools in one of the towns in South Carolina where my story takes place. I contacted one of the local newspapers there by phone and email, telling them of my upcoming school visit to their middle school. I sent them a news release about the new book, a cover letter, and a copy of the book.

The day of my author visit, a reporter showed up with a camera and interviewed me. Even though it was a small local periodical, I am able to include copies of that story in my marketing materials. Not all school visits are worthy of a news story, but sometimes it works. Just don't make a pest of yourself with the local media, as that can backfire. Be selective about contacting them.

An author visit is the first step in generating revenue from a school. Once you've established a good relationship with a school through a successful author visit, many of them will invite you back again and again. There are some schools where I do author visits to their fourth graders each year—a whole new group of students. That's one of the unique aspects of selling books to schools. You've got a brand-new audience each year.

And last but certainly not least, remember to send a thank-you note to your school contact within a few days after your visit. Many of the teachers will also have the students write thank-you notes to you. Acknowledge their letters with a personal note and let the teachers know how much you enjoyed interacting with their students.

Add all of these educators' names to your school contact list. Hopefully, they have agreed to be added to your distribution list of any emails, blogs, or newsletters you send out. Nurturing these relationships that you've already established can be instrumental in creating additional opportunities for you in the future.

Chapter 4

Preparing
for an Author Visit

After you've scheduled an author visit to a school, establish good communication with the person who will be coordinating your visit. It's good to clarify in writing what your fee will be and if you will be able to sell your books to students.

I had a problem once when a principal agreed to my fee but he retired before my visit took place; the bookkeeper was hesitant to pay me because the new principal had not agreed to it. Luckily, I had an email paper trail with the arrangement that the first principal had agreed to. The new principal authorized the payment without question.

Some authors create a contract to be signed by their contact or the person who will authorize payment. I have not done that because I've found it sometimes intimidates teachers, media specialists, or bookkeepers. So I keep it simple. However, I do make sure everything is spelled out in an email, and I print a copy of it and take it with me on the day of my visit. I've never had a problem.

In your early discussions with your contact, emphasize that your visit will be more meaningful for the students if they are familiar with your book. That will encourage them to purchase copies for the school. Ideally they will purchase one or two classroom sets so the students themselves can read the books, thus promoting literacy.

However, with school budgets being tight, they might only purchase enough for each teacher at a specific grade level to have one copy. I suggest that the teachers read a few chapters each day after lunch. It's a good way to invest some valuable class time while the students are experiencing that post-lunch weariness. It also gets the teachers familiar with your book.

You should confirm your visit with your contact at least a week before the event. Ask for specific directions to the school if you are not familiar with where it is, and ask where you should park your car. If you plan to be on the campus at the end of the day, you may want to park your car in a place where you can leave easily. Otherwise you could get caught in the after-school pickup traffic.

Selling Books to Students

About a week before your visit, send your contact a student book order form so these can be sent home to the parents. This has to be done before your visit, or the students will not come prepared with money to purchase your books on the day of your presentation. I suggest you offer a discount to students, in which case you will title it a Student Discount Book Order Form. When possible, I design it so two order forms can be printed on one sheet of paper, thus saving the school some paper. They will cut the sheets in half and give them to the students.

I write the form in the third person, stating that "Author Jane R. Wood will be visiting our school on XYX date." I give a short blurb about the educational value of my books and mention some of the awards they have received. I state that if any students would like to purchase their own copies of my books, I will sign and personalize them for each student. Then I list the books and the price, with a place for them to check which books they want.

I also include spaces for them to print the student's name and their teacher's name. That way, if I'm asked to sign the books before or after my presentation, those forms can be placed in each book and it will identify to which teacher the books should be delivered. If the school has allowed enough time, I prefer to sign the books at the end of each presentation so I can meet each student who buys one. I like the personal contact.

It's always good to make this purchasing process as teacher-friendly as possible. I suggest to my contact that any student who wants to buy a book, bring their order form and cash or check sealed in an envelope and give it directly to me. That way the teachers can collect the sealed envelopes in the days before my visit, but they don't have to touch any of the money. The teachers distribute the envelopes back to the students before my presentation.

If you are signing the books when the students are present, ask to have an adult volunteer assist you in collecting the money. That way, you can focus on personalizing the books for each of the students and interacting with them.

You will have to decide if you're willing to accept checks. I've received a few bad checks over the years, but the amounts were so small that it has not been an issue for me. I consider it a part of the cost of doing business.

Another option that works well for some schools is when the school collects all the money in advance and writes me one check. I sell the books to the school at a discount, cheaper than the price directly to students,

because I don't have to pay state sales tax on sales to schools. In that case, the school can "sell" the books to the students at an increased price, and use the difference to help pay for my author visit.

There are many other options that can be offered. Some authors donate a number of books to the school, but then charge full price to the students. Everything is negotiable. I've found it's best to establish your own policies, put them in writing on your website and flier, and also when you email a school about a potential visit. If you need to negotiate something different, do so in a way that makes sense for both of you.

I will admit that I sometimes do author visits to schools for free when they are local and do not require any major travel. I ask that I be allowed to sell books to the students. Sometimes I don't sell a lot of books, but that's the risk I take. If restaurants can offer dinner specials and retail stores create discount coupons, I figure I can offer discounts to schools when it makes sense.

As an example, the retail price of my books is $8.99. I sell them to students at a discount of $8.00 and to schools for $7.00. Keeping the numbers simple also makes it easy for my record-keeping. And offering my books at an affordable price is important when I'm selling to schools and students.

Details Regarding Your Author Visit

A few other details that you should discuss with your school contact before your visit:

- What is your schedule for the day, and when should you arrive?
- How many presentations do they expect you to do?
- What will be the size of each group?
- What grade levels will you be presenting to? Will it be a mixed audience?

- Where will you be presenting? (a classroom, media center, auditorium);
- Any audio/visual needs you might require (laptop, projector, microphone); and
- Any other items you might need (flip chart, table, chair, water bottle).

You should also clarify when you will be signing books, as that can impact your schedule. Ask to allow at least a 15-minute break between sessions if you're going to do multiple presentations.

Sometimes the school will invite you for lunch. I've had lunches with teachers and administrators, but my favorite time is when I'm asked to join a group of students for lunch. Some schools will make it a celebration for the students who have read the most books. It's always a treat for the students and me.

Once you've confirmed your school visit, you should list it on your website's home page, calendar, or upcoming events page. Teachers and students often get excited when they see their school's name listed on your website. It's also good marketing when other schools check out your website and see that you've got other school visits scheduled. You can also promote it on any social media to which you belong. I usually post something on Facebook on the week of a school visit, and then I share a photograph from that school the day after my visit. It's all about creating buzz and making people aware of your activity. Who knows? One of your Facebook friends might help you schedule a visit at another school.

One other piece of information you should explore with your contact regards school security. Schools will require you to check in at the main office. If you've been given instructions to park in a convenient place not close to the main office, you still need to go to the main office and officially sign in. Make sure you have a photo ID with you.

Many schools will require that you remain in the company of school personnel while you are on their campus. Some school districts may ask you to have a background check done that requires fingerprints. (In Florida, refer to the Jessica Lunsford Act.)

Find out what the rules are in advance and respect them. They will protect both you and the school.

Generating Excitement About Your Author Visit

Schools will often promote your visit in their newsletter to parents and on their website. It's always fun to drive up to a school and see your name on the marquee. It all helps to build momentum for a successful connection with the students, parents, and the community surrounding the school.

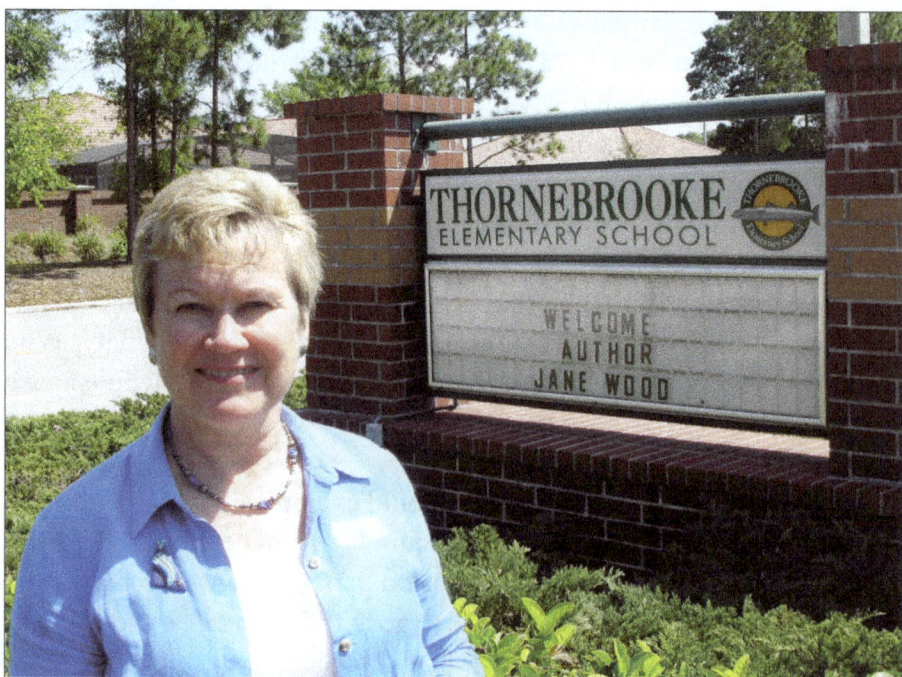

Your goal is to generate as much excitement as you can about your up-coming visit. I always ask if there is something specific the teachers would like me to include in my presentation. I make sure they know about the educational resources on my website. I also offer to share some ways that other schools have made my author visits more exciting.

Some schools have created artwork about one of my stories and posted it along the hallways. Others have had students dress up as some of the characters in my books. One media specialist prepared recipes from dish-es mentioned in my book and other foods that are representative of the setting of my story.

Freedom Shores Elementary School in Boynton Beach, Florida, involved the whole school, including administrators and parents, in a study of two of my books. Media Specialist Michelle Cates had students drawing maps,

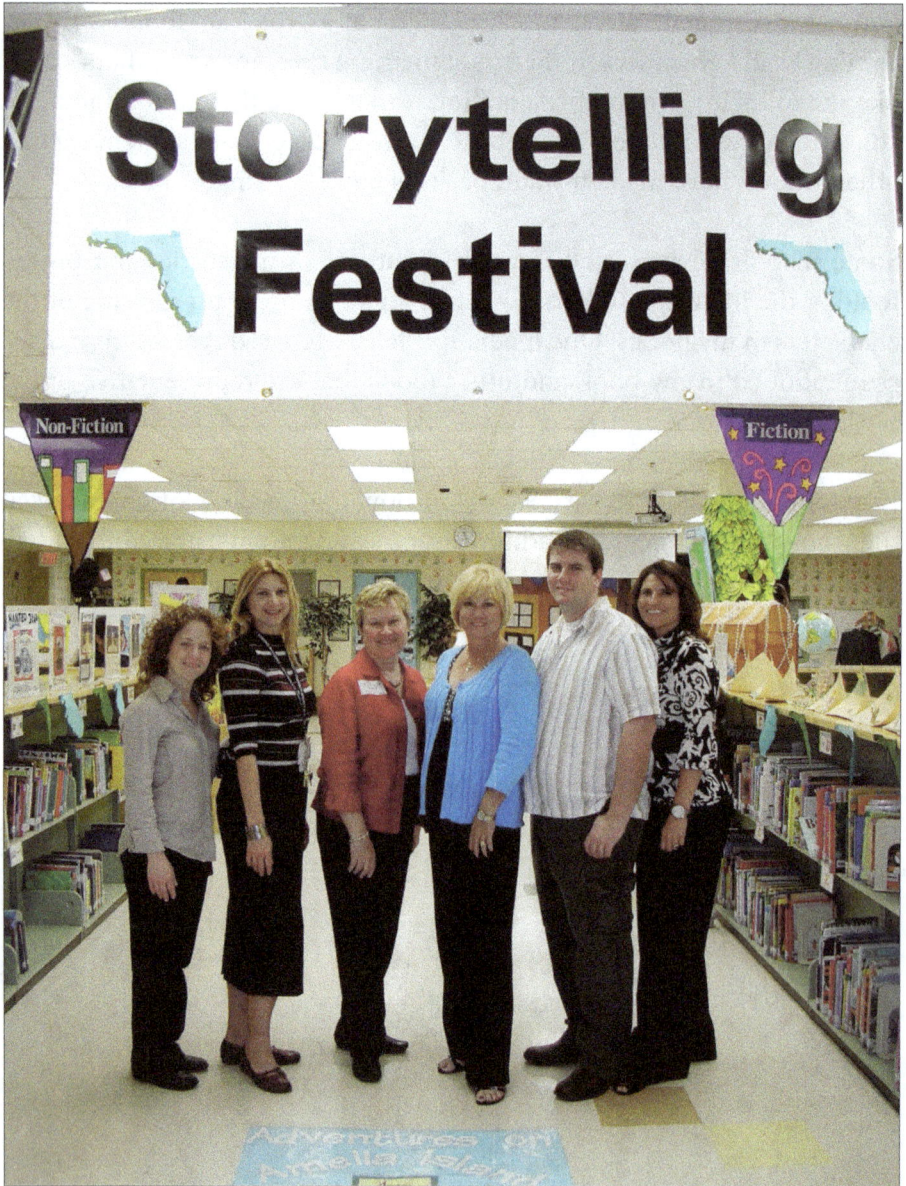

producing videos, and acting out dramatizations from my stories. Music teacher Brett Ovcen wrote an original song about my books and had the kids sing it to me. That was a real thrill!

One year the principal at Freedom Shores made comments on the school's intranet, discussing parts of the book with students and parents throughout the week. They make reading a serious yet fun activity at that school. According to Michelle Cates:

> *Author visits create the personal connection between students and a story during a "one book read." When a school invests instructional time and funds to share a single book, student motivation soars. This immersion elevates the author to celebrity status. In addition to an assembly presentation, authors sign books and take souvenir pictures with students. For the past six years of our Florida Storytelling Festival, meeting the author is the climax of our program. What better way to fulfill the students' excitement than to meet the author and to personally ask questions? The author visit experience contributes to a lifelong love of reading and a school culture celebrating literacy.*

It would be wonderful if more schools would generate that kind of excitement for reading. With your help, they can.

Chapter 5

Developing Your School Presentation

Rule number one is to know your audience. Create a presentation that is age appropriate. Rule number two is you must be comfortable interacting with kids.

If you're speaking to younger students, say kindergarten through second grade, you've got to keep it short, usually about 30 minutes. Otherwise the wiggle factor kicks in. With younger students it's also advisable to utilize a variety of approaches.

A strong introduction to the subject matter is important, as it helps them focus on what you're going to be talking about. Show them that you're happy to be there. Your enthusiasm will be contagious. Be careful about becoming too interactive with this age group, as every one of them will have something they want to share with you. Photographs, visual aids, and props are especially good for younger groups.

I show photographs of people, places, and animals that are featured in my books. I usually share my book, *Trouble on the St. Johns River*,

Peter M. Rose, Save the Manatee Club

with this age group, as I have many pictures of manatees and sea turtles. Kids this age love animals, and it gives me an opportunity to share an environmental message.

Of course, to have these kinds of visual presentations, you need photographs that relate to the content of your book. I take most of my own photographs, but if I use someone else's photos, I always obtain permission from them and credit them if their photos are used in my book.

I limit the number of photographs for this age group, and vary my presentation strategy so the youngsters won't get bored. It's good to allow a few questions at the end, but be aware that they're capable of asking you anything. Be prepared to deal with any awkward questions in a diplomatic way. Teachers will usually come to your rescue, as well.

For upper elementary and middle school students, I also talk about how and why I write my books. I spend some time discussing the writing process, with special emphasis on revising and rewriting. (Teachers love it when you talk about this.) And I include anything else that the teachers have asked me to emphasize.

Another way I make my presentation more meaningful is to make it personal. Students like to hear how I got started in writing. I talk about my third-grade teacher who asked us to write a poem, and how I fell in love with the magic of words at the age of eight. I talk about my sons, who became the models for two of the characters in my books, sometimes sharing humorous anecdotes about their escapades. Kids love this!

I talk about my love of history—born in a town in Oregon near where Lewis and Clark ended their historic expedition; about growing up near the Kennedy Space Center and watching America's journeys into space; and traveling to historic sites in this country and around the world. Sharing these details about my life explains why I like to weave history into my stories, and also helps them connect to me as a real person.

"It's a powerful moment when you see children make a connection between the words on the page and the author ... bringing them to life. It's one thing for kids to read books, but the chance to meet the authors and hear what it's like to write a book, that's an experience they'll remember for a lifetime."

—Clare Dubase, Media Specialist

As authors, we are storytellers. By incorporating some personal stories into our presentation, we are creating a stronger connection between the writer and the reader. Hopefully, students will want to learn more about some of their favorite authors, stimulating some additional reading on their part.

Speaking to older students becomes a little more academic. I've had high school creative writing teachers invite me to speak to their classes about the writing process and what is involved in publishing a book. So even if your book does not match any particular subject in a school's curricula, you can be a candidate to talk to English and creative writing classes. A good person to contact at a high school would be the head of the English department.

Make It Visual

For upper elementary grades and middle school, I use a PowerPoint presentation which includes photographs of the places featured in my books, such as the photo of The Pirates' House taken in Savannah for my book, *Ghosts on the Coast: A Visit to Savannah and the Low Country.*

Because I weave history into four of my stories, my hope is to make the history of a given area more relevant to the students because they see it as a real place. Many students who do not like to read a social studies textbook will relate to history when it's part of a story.

For my book *Trouble on the St. Johns River,* which has an environmental theme, I include photos of manatees and sea turtles, as well as some pictures of the places my characters in the book visit. They're all real places—a research reserve, a sea turtle rehabilitation center, and a museum of science and history. As an added bonus, all of these places have sold my books in their gift shops. But the real payoff for me is when I meet a family that tells me they visited one of these places because their child read my book.

I spend a lot of time creating my presentations and will try to customize them to each school. I carry my PowerPoint presentation on a USB flash drive, and request that the school provide a laptop and LCD projector. It's nice when you can travel light, especially if you're going to be taking books with you. Invest in a wheeled carrier so you can schlep the books into the school without breaking your back. Remember to bring two good signing pens, and it's good to have a paper notepad available so you can write out the correct spelling of a student's name before you personalize it in the book. The spelling of some names can be challenging.

During a school presentation I usually discuss only one book, but sometimes schools request that I speak about two or more. I have developed multiple presentations, so I can accommodate whatever the school requests.

Because I store them all on one USB flash drive, I'm prepared if there's a last-minute change in what they want me to talk about.

I also have a backup plan in case I am not able to do the presentation I had planned for that day. Sometimes the audio/visual equipment does not work, or the electricity goes out, or my scheduled time slot gets shortened because of a fire drill. I've learned to be flexible.

You might have to improvise, so it's good to have a Plan B. Sometimes I read excerpts from the book that are especially visual or humorous; or share some interesting anecdotes of things that have happened to me as an author; or I extend the question-and-answer time. The key is to still provide a meaningful program for the students, even when the conditions are not ideal.

Make It Interactive

I ask students to hold their questions until the end, as I will leave time for them when I'm finished. If you allow students to ask questions during your presentation, you will never get through it all. Frequently, teachers will have the students prepare questions in advance and then will designate certain students to ask them. That way, the teachers can identify the most significant things they want discussed, and you don't waste time on trivial comments.

Elementary students like to talk about their personal experiences, and your presentation may trigger some memories they feel compelled to share. During the Q&A part of your author visit, it's good to state that you are interested in their questions, not their stories. The teachers will often help enforce this. Suggest they ask you questions about things they'd like to know more about. Also, include students from different parts of the room, not only those in the front row or those who wave their hands frantically in front of you.

You can pretty much anticipate the kinds of questions that will be asked, so it's good to prepare your answers in advance. I always like to have a few personal anecdotes to share, as well, since it makes the students feel more connected to me.

Your goal is to make your presentation as engaging as possible. A room full of middle school kids is a tough crowd. Some authors will read an excerpt from their book—the more dramatic, the better. Others have developed clever poems they recite at the beginning of their presentation to get the students' attention. Some authors like to dress in a costume, use a variety of hats, or have some props that relate to their book.

Authors with good singing voices will often sing an original song related to their story. Songs that are interactive and get the students responding musically can fire up a room. (Just be careful what you wish for. It's best to save these activities near the end of your presentation.)

And I've seen illustrators totally amaze a room full of youngsters as they sketch a whimsical character or make a scene from a book come alive visually. Sometimes authors will co-present with the illustrators of their books. That's a win-win for the students, especially if the presenters can demonstrate how the two must work together, a desirable life skill as well as one that is identified in most state standards. Who knows how many budding artists or writers might be inspired to pursue their own creative goals?

Whatever kind of presentation you develop, it must be something you are comfortable doing. You're not just there to sell books; you're there to share your passion for writing and give students a peek into the world of an author.

You might be the first author some students have met. If you make a positive impression on them, you may stimulate their interest in reading more books. Authors of children's books have a responsibility to do that.

On that note, another suggestion I would make is that you become familiar with other books in your genre, especially those on the best-seller lists and the state and school reading lists. Students will often ask if you are familiar with a particular book or with other authors. It's always good when you can mention one or two that you've read. You will be endorsing reading. I feel strongly that we have a responsibility to promote literacy to young readers, regardless of whether it's our own books or someone else's. The educators will appreciate that too.

The next important step justifies my repeating it here: Remember to send a thank-you note to your school contact within a few days after your visit. Many of the teachers will also have the students write thank-you notes to you. Add all of these educators to a school contact list. Hopefully, they have agreed to be added to your distribution list of any emails, blogs, or newsletters you send out. You'd be surprised how many schools will want to schedule a return visit in the future.

Chapter 6

Developing Other Presentations

Virtual Author Visits

I've done virtual author visits to schools for years, connecting with schools in many different states and countries. When the COVID-19 pandemic hit in 2020, it drastically changed the way schools operated. Students were no longer meeting in classrooms but were doing virtual learning from home. Teachers were challenged to provide meaningful learning experiences using electronic devices.

Many new programs were developed to help accomplish that, and a variety of platforms were used by school districts to connect with their students. Just as educators were challenged to use technology to find new ways to teach, authors had to find new ways to reach out to students.

Some authors created book trailers, did virtual author interviews, performed a read-aloud, and created a variety of videos to attract students. I did a video tour of St. Augustine, visiting places featured in my book, *Voices in St. Augustine*. It was not up to Hollywood standards, but I had teachers tell me that students enjoyed seeing the places where my characters visited.

Some authors charge for virtual visits and others do them for free. In any event, your goal will be to expand your market and sell some books. In fact, you could make that a requirement of your agreeing to do a virtual visit with a school. As I mentioned before, your interaction with the students will be more meaningful for them if they are familiar with one of your books, so encourage the school to purchase some copies in advance of your presentation.

You should also ask for the opportunity to sell books directly to the students. You can use the same Student Discount Order Form that you've created for the school visits you do in person. Simply email it to the contact person in advance. They will have to collect the orders and the money and send them to you, but teachers want their students reading so it's usually not a concern.

I always test the connection with the school the day before my presentation. My presentation usually lasts from 30-45 minutes. Prepare a short presentation based on what you have discussed with the teachers. Sometimes I share photographs of the places featured in my books just like I do with the in-person presentations. And I always leave time for questions.

Ideally, the teachers will have had the students prepare their questions in advance. Depending on the size of the group and their location, students may have to step up to the camera so you can see and hear them. If you can't understand the student, ask the teacher to repeat the question. You can claim you can't hear well because of a weak connection, so as not to embarrass the student.

I do my virtual visits from my computer in my office. I aim the camera at my bookcases and not at my sometimes-cluttered desk. If you need any props or copies of your books, have them handy.

Distance learning will continue to play a role in how schools teach today, and school districts are still investing in the technology that facilitates its delivery. There is still a need for virtual author visits to schools especially when trying to connect with schools in a different state or country. It requires some advance planning and preparation but can allow you to reach classrooms and students anywhere in the world.

Speaking to Parents, Educators, and Other Groups

Other kinds of presentations you might want to develop are those for parents. All schools have some kind of parent organization that holds regular meetings, and they are often looking for speakers. As a published author you are in a perfect position to talk about the importance of reading. I always begin by introducing my five books, as that gives me credibility. Then I list some specific suggestions on how parents can encourage their children to become readers.

One of the most significant ways they can do that is by being readers themselves. It sounds so obvious, but with today's busy lifestyles many parents feel they don't have time to read. If they came to hear you speak, they're already interested in the education of their children. Remind them that they are important role models. When their kids see them reading, it sends a positive message. Other suggestions for parents can be found on numerous reading-related websites.

Speaking to educator groups can also be very valuable. I've spoken at media specialist conferences, reading councils, school faculties, and re-tired teachers' organizations. Don't forget about women's clubs and civic groups. They too are concerned about literacy among young people. You will need to customize your presentation to each group—they are also stakeholders in educating the next generation. Back-of-the-room sales can be very profitable when speaking to these groups.

You should consider presenting to other children's groups, such as sum-mer camps, after-school programs, reading clubs for kids sponsored by local libraries, and homeschool groups. Numerous nonprofit orga-nizations in each community sponsor programs for kids, like the Boy Scouts and Girl Scouts, Boys & Girls Clubs, church youth groups, and city-sponsored programs.

"Our school has offered a valuable enrichment program for our Extended Day students by offering book club chats with author Jane Wood. The students are engaged, their reading scores have improved, and their vocabulary and comprehension skills have increased."

—Donna Ayers, Extended Day Director

If you write books for kids, then your goal is to identify places where kids will be. You might want to donate a few copies of your book to some of these groups. Consider it part of your marketing budget. You never know when a donated book will land in the hands of someone who sees the value of purchasing more copies.

And even if your donation does not generate more sales for you, you've provided something valuable to a group that is concerned about the future of the young people they serve. We all have a stake in that!

Chapter 7

Making Money Selling to Schools

I've talked about how to find schools, how to promote your books to schools, how to schedule and prepare an author visit, and now comes a critical part—how to get paid.

I make money three ways when I market to schools. First, I can receive an honorarium for doing an author visit. Second, the school orders books so the students will become familiar with them before my visit. Third, the students want to purchase their own copies of my books.

You need to create an invoicing system. There are software programs, like *QuickBooks*, that can accommodate that for you, or there are websites that will provide invoice templates you can use. Schools need paperwork to purchase books and to pay you a speaking fee.

Remember, when you're dealing with schools, make the bookkeeper your best friend. That person holds the purse strings. Many of them will require an invoice in advance of an author visit. If so, provide it. Most schools will give you a check on the day of your visit.

Some schools will pay you with funds that reside with the school district. In that case, you will be given a purchase order (PO). When that happens, you should create an invoice, listing the PO number, and send it to the address designated on the purchase order.

Purchase orders can sometimes take a while to remit. Be patient. If you're not willing to wait or can't deplete your inventory waiting for payment, then you should probably not do business with a school that requires that process. You don't want to alienate the school bookkeeper or the financial personnel at the school district by badgering them about payment.

You may also be asked to become a vendor for the school district. The requirements vary from district to district, but it's a good idea to pursue this if you intend to market your books to many schools in a given district.

Check out the school district's website to apply to become a vendor. This is usually located in the purchasing department.

Sometimes schools will pay with a credit card. If you don't accept credit cards, perhaps you can use PayPal. Again, there are expenses involved in using either of these methods, but it's all a part of doing business. Not having payment options available to your customers can drastically limit your sales, not to mention your credibility as a professional.

Sometimes schools will be very slow in paying. That depends on who received the invoice and when they processed it. There have been times (if it's been more than six weeks) when I've had to call a bookkeeper to ask when I can expect payment. Usually it means a media specialist or a teacher did not submit my invoice. A phone call or friendly reminder via email can usually produce results.

One other thing you need to secure from any schools you do business with is their tax exemption certificate or number. You are not responsible for paying state sales taxes on sales to schools, but if you ever get audited you may have to produce that information. You will be responsible for paying sales tax on student sales since they are not tax exempt. I make the discount price to students an even number so I don't have to deal with coins, but I take the sales tax figure into account.

Travel Expenses

Another thing to consider when scheduling school visits is your travel expenses. I charge for these when I travel more than 100 miles from my home. I use the IRS rate for mileage and per diem rates for lodging, meals, and incidentals. And of course, all of that is negotiable. One school I visited had a local motel as their business partner. They made arrangements for my lodging at that motel, which saved them money.

Whenever possible I will schedule several school visits in one geographic area so I can prorate the travel costs. I am not trying to make additional money off the schools by charging extra for my travel costs; I merely want to cover my expenses. Often, to limit their expenses, the first school that schedules me for an author visit will help me find additional schools in their area.

Note: Keeping receipts for all of your book-related expenses is essential. Any expenses that are not reimbursed to you can be used as deductions on your income tax returns for that year if you itemize. Consult a financial professional for guidance on what expenses may be eligible.

Sources of Funding for Author Visits

Generating revenue from schools all depends on their ability to pay. Frequently the media specialist will have money in his or her budget to fund the purchase of books or pay for an author visit. In that case, it's good to market yourself early in the school year since those funds are usually limited. I've had schools tell me they had already booked an author and spent all their money for that year.

Sometimes the principal or the reading specialist will have some discretionary funds. I've also had parent groups underwrite my author visits. School advisory councils are also interested in providing extra resources for the school, and some schools will approach a business partner for support.

Often, educational foundations or other local nonprofit organizations will sponsor grants for schools or teachers. I've had many schools purchase classroom sets of my books by using grant monies. They often use copies of my educational resources as part of their grant application. There are larger grants that schools can apply for, but they are usually tied to large projects that impact many students.

One author friend had a large number of his books purchased for a school through a men's civic club. That group also funded his author visit and travel expenses to a school some distance from his home.

I once received a large order for my book, *Trouble on the St. Johns River,* from a state environmental protection agency that was providing copies to science teachers in a specific area. Of course, I then followed up with the schools in that district to offer author visits to their schools.

In 2014, a large school district in Florida purchased 6,400 copies of my book, *Voices in St. Augustine.* Every fourth grader in the district read it as part of their study of Florida history. My book was selected because many teachers who had used it in their classrooms since its original publication in 2004 had requested it. Again, I followed up with numerous author visits to many of those schools, making it a very profitable year for me.

Corporate funding is sometimes available. Many large companies will make a commitment each year to fund certain projects in their community. Do some research to see if any local companies have projects designated for education or literacy. You might find those kinds of commitments on an organization's website, or perhaps an article in the newspaper showing a contribution they've recently made. When schools tell you they can't afford to buy your books or schedule an author visit, suggest they contact one of those organizations.

When I was the community affairs manager for a large corporation, I often received calls from schools and nonprofit groups looking for funding for deserving projects. Whenever possible, I donated some money or tried to connect them with other sources of funding.

Educators are hired to teach and are not trained in how to raise money. And they don't have time to search for places to get funding. So identifying funding sources for them could be beneficial to both of you. However, remember that these requests need to come from the schools, not from an author. You can point them in the right direction, but they're the ones who should request the support.

Many organizations feel strongly about supporting their local schools. Whenever I speak to one of these groups or even to individual members of such groups, I always take the opportunity to suggest they support reading in their schools. Many of them don't have time to volunteer or mentor a student, but as an organization they can designate some funding to support these kinds of projects.

Remind them that it does take a village and any investment they make in a school is an investment in their community.

Closing Thoughts

In marketing your books to schools, the challenge for an author is to write books that have educational value, or to find that value in their existing books. Then that value must be communicated to educators. As with all marketing, "they don't know if you don't tell them."

Marketing to schools requires some unique strategies. I hope some of the suggestions I've included here will help you break into this challenging yet rewarding market.

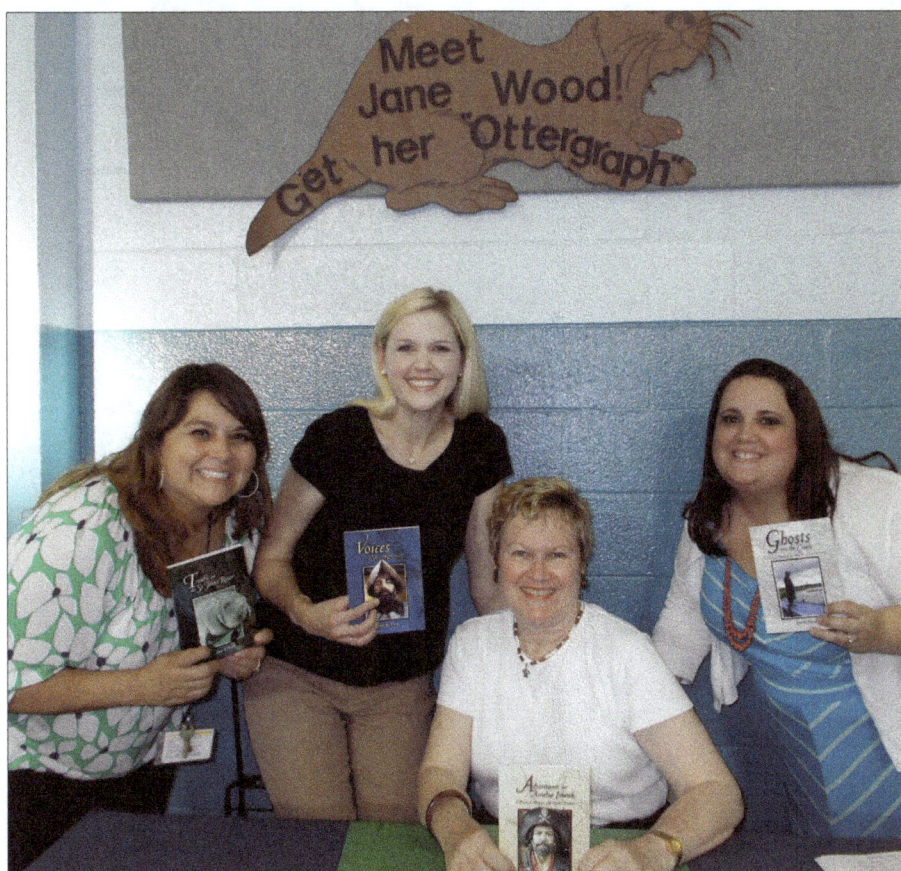

Resources Page

Accelerated Reader® – Suggest a Quiz
http://www.renaissance.com

Character Counts, Six Pillars
http://charactercounts.org/

Jane Wood's Books
www.janewoodbooks.com

Lexile Measures
http://www.lexile.com/

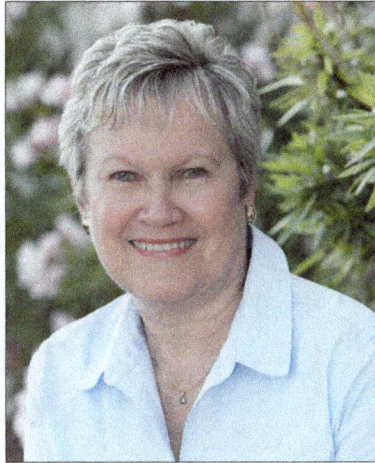

About the Author

J ane R. Wood is the author of five award-winning juvenile fiction books. She weaves history and science into stories filled with mystery and adventure. Young readers like her books because they're fun—teachers like them for their educational value.

Wood has an extensive background in marketing, community relations, and education. She uses her experience as a classroom teacher, newspaper reporter, and television producer in creating and promoting her books.

Wood earned a BA from the University of Florida and an MEd from the University of North Florida. She is an active member of the Florida Authors and Publishers Association, and has served on its board of directors since 2013. She is also an adjunct instructor at the University of North Florida, where she teaches classes on book publishing.

To learn more about Jane R. Wood and her books, visit her website at www.janewoodbooks.com.

Other Books by Jane R. Wood

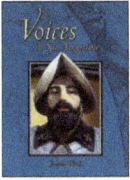

Voices in St. Augustine – Thirteen-year-old Joey Johnson hears voices, only he can't find the people who belong to them. His curiosity leads him on a quest where he learns more than just history about the Nation's Oldest City.

Adventures on Amelia Island: A Pirate, a Princess, and Buried Treasure – This book continues the escapades of the Johnson family. Local legends and tales of ghosts add to a story filled with colorful characters, humorous situations, and a youthful spirit of adventure.

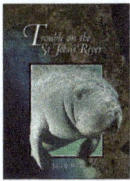

Trouble on the St. Johns River – After a close encounter with a manatee, a visit to a sea turtle center, and a family river tour, Joey, Bobby, and Katy decide to "do something" to try to make a difference in protecting endangered animals and preserving the environment.

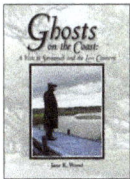

Ghosts on the Coast: A Visit to Savannah and the Low Country – It seems wherever they go, adventure follows the Johnson family. This time it comes when they visit Savannah, Charleston, and Pawleys Island, South Carolina—cities rich in history and ghost stories.

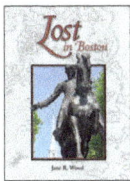

Lost in Boston – The Johnson family travels to Boston, where they explore several historic landmarks, including the Paul Revere House, the Old North Church, and the USS *Constitution*. New experiences and solving a crime add discovery and intrigue to this newest family adventure.

Books may be ordered at **www.janewoodbooks.com**.
Also available on Kindle and Nook.

www.ingramcontent.com/pod-product-compliance
Lightning Source LLC
LaVergne TN
LVHW021134080426
835509LV00010B/1355